THE SUCCESSFUL PRIVACY MINDSET

JACK NORTON

CONTENTS

FOREWORD: WHO IS THIS BOOK FOR AND WHY SHOULD YOU READ IT

BY SALLY COHEN

Coming home from my twenty first birthday party in downtown Chicago, I was attacked. That was the first time violence from a stranger had ever been inflicted on me - but sadly it wasn't the last time.

Several years later I met a very nice man that volunteered his time to edit a short film I had directed.

(Don't worry this film editor isn't my friend Jack Norton who wrote this book, and asked that I write this introduction).

This man and I worked together for several days side by side. I felt safe and he put me at ease. Little did I know that the few days we spent together on this simple film project would send my life in a direction I could never have imagined. My film premiered in Chicago - and my editor was in the audience there to support me along with my friends, family and everyone that helped out on the film. I didn't see his behavior as weird (at this point). However, I began to get alarmed when he would show up at festival screenings in the various towns my film and I traveled to. He "surprised" me with his "support" in Detroit, Milwaukee and Minneapolis. The biggest shock was when my film was invited to SXSW and guess who again "surprised" me with his "support"? You guessed it! My editor had driven all the way from Chicago, Illinois to Austin, Texas!

As most of the cases of stalkers go, our relationship escalated rapidly. We had become Facebook friends during our initial days of editing together. However, somehow he found out my favorite coffee shop, and from there followed me home - and now knew where I lived. What's more, he showed up on the set of the next film I was shooting. How he knew where our location was, well - when I found out how he knew - I was beyond shocked!

Eventually, when I confronted him with my worries and explained that I felt we needed some time away from each other, he became verbally abusive. His temper was terrifying. That's when the real insanity began: he started to write letters to my family and friends. He showed up to my best friend's work and refused to leave until she talked to me on his behalf. One night, I arrived back from a shoot - and - he was waiting for me in my apartment! Thankfully, I live just three blocks from a police station and cops were on hand within a minute of my call.

To make a very, very long and detailed story short, this man consumed my entire life for nearly two years. Eventually, after the legal system all but failed me (I had a restraining order which he repeatedly ignored), I decided to take matters into my own hands. I began to study all of the books, blog postings and news articles I could find on privacy. I became a student of YouTube tutorials on safety, self defense and common sense privacy for the digital age.

My friend Jack Norton and his wife Kitty have a similar story to mine, actually their story may be even more terrifying. They wrote an entire book about their adventure called *Two Stalkers One Goal*. I highly, highly recommend it! Jack goes into detail about surviving their horrific ordeal.

I actually "met" Jack and Kitty online via a

privacy message board forum on the "darkweb". After trading tips and tricks with each other online, eventually we met in person and have since all become close friends.

I know this book is a labor of love for Jack - and you can tell. He painstakingly details so much important, life saving information in this work.

It has been almost four years since the night I decided to take control of my safety and take back my life. Like Jack and his wife Kitty, I have learned a lot along the way. I just wish I had this book years ago! Jack's desire to share with you what steps they have done in order to protect themselves physically, digitally and mentally is inspiring.

Like Jack and Kitty, my story is a crazy one which no one should have to live through. Yet, I did.

You may wonder how my stalker knew my every location? The answer is simple - in those early days of our time together editing that film, I showed him a photo on my phone of the new kitten I had just adopted. While he pretended to be looking at that picture, he download an app which essentially "cloned" my phone and enabled him to see every email, text, photo, video - almost everything I ever did on my smartphone!

Seriously, I had no idea that any of this was happening. But it did.

It happened to me. And it can happen to you too.

This book covers practical tips and tricks about privacy. Not everything will apply to you - I suggest reading the entire book and making notes for steps you can take to make yourself safer immediately. Pick and choose what works best for you, given your situation.

When Jack asked me to write the introduction to this book, I jumped at the chance. The only thing he asked me to let readers know is that he has no background in law enforcement or the military. He is not a survivalist nor is he a hacker. Also, he is not a lawyer - so understand this book is simply documenting the tips he learned along his journey to becoming safe from his stalker.

I got many, many good ideas from reading this book. Everything that works for me, may not work for you - but I guarantee that if you follow some of the tips and tricks in this book, you will be safer than 99% of the rest of the population.

This book is for anyone that has ever felt

watched, ever felt that their privacy has been compromised or for anyone that has ever felt less than safe and secure. You deserve to feel safe at all times! That's the mantra I kept repeating to myself over and over: *you deserve to feel safe at all times!* It's true for me - and it's true for you.

If you are a survivor of an assault, rape, mugging, stalker, identity theft, home invasion or any other ugliness - there will be ideas in this book that will make you feel safe. One of the most troubling things about crime is that the victim can feel the scars for years and years afterwards. Jack told me simply in an email: *"My goal for readers of this book is to help switch you out of the victim mindset and into the survivor mindset!"*

It's time to take back your life. I know you can.

You deserve to feel safe at all times!

Shalom,

Sally Cohen

Chicago, Illinois

"I give the fight up:
let there be an end, a privacy,
an obscure nook for me.
I want to be forgotten...
even by God."

- Robert Browning, poet and playwright

PART I

Safety In The Shadows - The Ultimate Goal: Invisibility

In this chapter we will outline our ultimate goal - invisibility. We will realize that there is safety in the shadows. That freedom, true freedom, can only be found when privacy is strong.

We will discuss the mindset of stalkers and how to beat them.

And finally, we will begin to create our new life. It may be a new identity all together, or it may simply be taking the life you and currently living and building a fortress around it - so you can have a good life and be safe while doing so.

Either way, our adventure together starts now - so let's go!

Let's state this right from the beginning. Once I decided to take back the control I had lost and reclaim my life I became obsessed with privacy. I now have one goal, it is:

The ultimate goal is to make yourself invisible.

That's pretty understandable, but to be clear - by "invisible" I don't mean to become a hermit that never leaves the house, I mean to live a full, happy, adventurous life - only allowing the people that have earned my trust to know my real, true identity.

I can count on one hand that people in my life that I trust fully. These are people I would trust with my life. Only these people know my true identity. Every one else knows me, but they don't know the real me - so in a sense I have made myself "invisible" to these outsiders.

This is not a sad place to live - in fact, there is so much happiness and joy knowing that my private life is private, that I can take great comfort in my invisibility.

Would you rather be rich or famous?

To me this is a silly question - of course I would rather be rich, because the more money you have the more resources you have for safety and security (among other things). If your answer to this question is that you would rather be famous, you will have a hard time with many aspects of this book. You can still apply most of the concepts, tips and tricks - but to truly benefit and be safe you must let go of the idea of fame and embrace the idea of invisibility. There is true safety in the shadows.

Privacy Is Freedom

I personally believe that "freedom" can only be found in privacy. You are only free as long as you are not being watched, tracked, monitored and easily accessible.

If you fight for your absolute right to privacy, then you too can enjoy the benefits of freedom. A free society is a private society. To live free in our current world is getting harder by the minute. As technology threatens to engulf us with unwanted (and mostly unauthorized) surveillance, the true patriot is the one that believes in the freedom of privacy. Fight for it.

Despite our digital age, privacy is still very obtainable.

There was a time, not so long ago, when I didn't think about privacy - I simply existed and followed all the waves of what is popular in the world today. I documented my entire existence on Facebook and Instagram, I even had a blog on YouTube in which I filmed my entire personal life! Those days are over. But do you know what? I am able to enjoy my life on a deeper level. A feeling of contentment has flooded my soul knowing that I am an advocate for my own privacy and that with each step I take I am becoming more free - and there is true safety in that freedom.

Freedom first: everything else comes second.

The first step I took was to stop defining myself as a "victim". Instead, I began to think of myself as a "survivor" or even a "warrior". How exciting is it to define yourself as a "warrior"? That is what you are! You beat your attacker and the proof is that you are here today reading this book. Now, it's time for a little vigilante justice - I personally believe that the best revenge for a stalker is to cut off their supply, and go invisible. They will know that I am still alive having a great, happy, joyful and prosperous life without them. Knowing that will torture them. As a warrior my goal is to torture my opponent. I do this by fighting for my right to privacy.

The Levels Of Privacy

There are many levels to this fight for privacy. I went to a fairly extreme level. For you it may be as simple as to Tweet less. That's fine too. Whatever place you fall on the spectrum of privacy is entirely your choice. I do not want to label the levels of privacy, because there are enough labels placed upon people in this world.

I consider a very basic idea whenever I am making a choice in my life now. Perhaps, it will give you insight into which level of privacy I am now living on. Every decision, action or opportunity I am presented with I ask myself one basic question: *Can I remain invisible and therefore keep myself free?* If the answer is "yes" then I proceed with caution being careful to move gingerly through the opportunity. If the answer is "no" I walk away and never look back.

If "Option A" poses a threat to your privacy and therefore puts your freedom in jeopardy, then you must walk away from "Option A" and consider "Option B". Or "Option C". Or "Option D". And so on.

Anonymity Is Essential - The Idea Behind Anonymity

For my journey into the world of personal

privacy I learned early on that anonymity is absolutely essential.

But what is "anonymity". It does sound vague.

The easiest to understand definition I have found is that *anonymity is keeping your actions and activities separate from your true identity or an identity that is publicly known.*

The Greek word "anonymia" literally means "without a name" or "nameless".

I love the concept of anonymity. I have several "identities" that I identify myself with:

1.My legal government identity

2.My personal identity which is known by the friends and family members I trust with my life

3.My professional identity as an author

4.My professional identity as an artist

5.My personal identity which is known by friends and associates that I love and care about, but I do not trust with my life

I also have dozens more names which I use for unimportant things online and offline. None of these names I would consider part of my identity.

If you are an artist or creative person you should look into the concept of "obscurantism" - which basically is deliberate obscurity for the purposes of literature or art. This theory within art history gave birth to the concept of a "pen name".

Over the years, artists have found that "pen names" have numerous benefits. When the artist remain anonymous there is an added element of mystique to their world. It also avoids interest being focused on the artist instead of the work. Most true artists would rather the focus of attention be on their work and not on their personal life.

Finally there is a psychological effect of using a pen name which may be seen as beneficial. A pen name removes the impact your actions or work may have on your reputation. In other words, your creativity is less censored because you are "hiding" in the safety of a pseudonym.

Basic Privacy Tips

Before I began to fall down the rabbit hole of creating multiple identities and personas, I decided to follow a few basic privacy tips to keep me safe from my stalker. He was becoming increasingly violent - making very troubling threats and so the following were some of my earliest steps in living a safer life.

First, I have a camera on me at all times. Not my smartphone (which I got rid of and I'll tell you why later in this book). No, a real camera. When I am in public I wear mine around my neck at all times. Yes, this is kind of nerdy and I do look like a tourist, however many studies have shown that criminals on all levels will actively avoid a camera so I wear one. I also know that if my stalker were to show up I could immediately film our confrontation. I know the fear of prison is a good deterrent for this coward, and video evidence of an assault would certainly be compelling footage in the courtroom. So, I wear a camera everywhere I go in public. A side benefit is that I have become a much better photographer simply by wanting to take pictures of interesting things I see throughout my day.

I have a photo blog and post new pictures all day long. As a side hustle I also sell prints on canvas of my photos. I do all this under a pen name and no one knows that my work is by me.

Despite being a night owl, I try to always shop in the daytime and when crowds are at their peek. I always try to remain in crowds because stalkers tend to avoid doing anything extreme while in a crowd - because they will get caught.

I never go to an isolated place. Period. I also never drive on isolated roads - I make sure to follow busy roads with lots of traffic. I also avoid driving at night.

A huge tip I put into practice was to stop connecting my real legal government name with my real date of birth. This is especially dangerous to do online. I simply began to give out multiple different dates for my birthday - I changed the day, month and year. It took about three years to permeate online, but now if you search my legal name you will see a date of birth that is completely inaccurate. Actually, depending on what search engine you use or what website you land on, you will find conflicting dates of birth all over the internet. This is very, very good.

I stopped using the real last four digits of my social security number to identify me with business and services. You know how you are always asked for the last four digits of your social? Well, I just pick four random digits and use those whenever I am asked.

Did you know that there are "Burner Social Security Numbers"? There are. They are 987-65-4320 through 987-65-4329. Use them and you will never be using someone else's identity: because these numbers have never been issued to anyone, and never will be.

I removed my real resume and my real bio from online. There are way too many personal details which are exposed when posting your bio and resume online. LinkedIn is especially dangerous. Stalkers can - and will - use schools you listed as a starting point to befriend your old classmates. Using a false profile they will impersonate a classmate and then friend you. That means you - and your old classmates - will all be friends with someone they think is a former classmate but in reality is your stalker! No bueno. Identity thieves also love LinkedIn and use your real resume to began the process of opening up new credit cards in your name - or trying to access your bank account. Delete all real facts about your resume and bio online immediately! At least I did.

I never show my drivers license as identification - unless I am driving and a police officer stops me. I only use my passport as my ID in all situations. Why? Because driver's licenses have your address on them - but a passport does not. So if you frequent bars in your neighborhood, and you use your drivers license as an ID, guess what? Your stalker could easily give a bartender ten bucks to memorize your address. They can't get that info from your passport!

I got rid of all my discount and membership club cards. Businesses use them for targeted marketing, which means my spending habits are tracked and sold to other companies. A profile is kept on me and my stalker could find out my purchasing habits if they were able to access any of my discount or membership club cards.

Finally, I stopped voting. If you are a registered voter your address will be linked to your name in thousands of databases which are easily accessible online. My freedom doesn't depend on who is my Senator, Congressman or even President. My freedom is solely found in privacy. Which means, in order to live a private life - I can never vote again.

Stalkers Are Sick, Assume The Worst

You can not think like your stalker. Because stalkers are sick - and you (I presume) are not. Stalkers are violent and will stop at nothing to have you in their life - on their own terms. Which, I promise, will most likely not be very pleasant.

I can't think like my stalker. But I can still be proactive and try to think like him. How? Simple. I assume the worst.

I assume the worst possible outcome for any

scenario I find myself in, and I based my actions accordingly.

Paranoia does not mean you are paranoid, it means you are aware.

The Gray Rock Always Wins - You Must Be Forgettable

After I had put these few steps into place my life immediately began to start to feel like my own. For so long I had felt like I had lost all control.

Then I discovered the "gray rock strategy" while watching a YouTube video late one night.

Basically the concept is simple: a gray rock is boring. A gray rock is forgettable. No one ever picks up a gray rock - they just pass right by it.

That is why a gray rock always wins. If you become a gray rock, if you become completely forgettable, you will win too.

How do you keep a low profile? By becoming a gray rock. By being forgettable, boring, totally uninteresting.

I made it my goal to become a gray rock. I will never have extreme hair color or piercings. I will never wearing unique or bright colored clothes. I changed my appearance to blend into the masses. My goal was to walk down a street and not be noticed. To simply become a gray rock.

My goal was to become a stranger - but never to be strange. I wanted to blend into a crowd, and use this to hide my identity. You simply can not stick our or be remembered in any way whatsoever. Act normal and stick to the background.

Remember: there is safety in the shadows. Just tell me this - when is the last time you have noticed and picked up a boring old gray rock?

Exactly.

How To Build The New You

This leads me to my next point. I decided to build a new me. Of course, my core identity remained the same. But to the outside world I started to shed anything that made me recognizable - my hobbies, my habits, my social circles. All of them I slowly began to change. More on this in a bit.

I already started to modify my appearance by becoming a gray rock. But I knew that to become completely private I must drastically alter my appearance.

If you have always been very skinny, try to gain ten pounds. If you are overweight, now is a great time to work on your physical appearance and health! As I mentioned, I now dress completely different from my old public self. I also stopped wearing my contacts and started wearing glasses. I got several tattoos.

Men have the advantage of growing facial hair. If you are a man, I would recommend using this gift.

When changing your personal appearance, start by throwing out all your old clothes. I do not recommend donating them because this may raise too many red flags to your pursuer - they will be on the lookout for you in new clothes, not good. I went to a store I have never shopped in and bought clothes I would have never worn before. I also started wearing a hat - I had never worn one before. Finally, I dyed my hair - not to some crazy color, but to a modest one I had never tried before.

I also started to use new mannerisms as a way to mask my old mannerisms as best as possible. One trick is to put a small pebble or tack in your shoe - it will force you to walk and stand differently.

I studied acting, because to be a successful actor your identity must change to its core.

One technique you learning in acting class is to create a character history or "backstory". This is kind of fun and you can do this for your new public persona. Some questions to consider:

Where are you from?

What did you do before your current job?

Where is your family from?

Where are they now?

What kind of foods do you enjoy?

What are your favorite bands?

Who is your favorite author?

I suggest you use my name when you answer that last question. Just kidding!

Seriously though, you must learn to act naturally as you answer these questions. Also - the idea is to change your answers to something completely unexpected. If you were a vegan, your stalker would never think to look for you at the local steakhouse! And so on.

The bottom line is that you create a new everything for yourself. Fun, huh? I think it is. This is life's way of letting you wipe the slate clean.

I have studied the Witness Protection Program and they have you work for three months on these three elements:

1. Practice your back story

2. Learn the specifics of where you are from (your "hometown")

3. Practice signing your new name

Over and over again for three months. That's

what the United States government has folks in the program practice. Interesting, no?

Keep in mind, you are not sentencing yourself to a life of isolation and despair. Making new friends is necessary. No matter what, neighbors and locals will always be a part of your life, and it's totally cool if you become friends with some of those folks - just make sure you do that under your new identity.

Don't be worried about meeting new people. They may even come in handy if you need them to verify your new identity and backstory a few years down the road. The only thing you must worry about is revealing your old identity to these new folks.

Predictability Is The Enemy

Predictability is defined as the consistent *repetition of a state, course of action, behavior, or the like, making it possible to know in advance what to expect.*

The one thing to always keep in mind is that predictability is the one trait that your stalker relies on most to effectively track you.

So, now is the time to become that wild and crazy guy that you always wanted to be - and start a life of spontaneity. Change your routine, your patterns and your habits. Immediately.

And once you do change from your old life into your new one, remember to never become comfortable and complacent, letting your new habits fall into such a place that they become your (new) old habits. Don't do it! Remain vigilant always - keep checking yourself, and do whatever it takes to avoid your old habits, routines and patterns.

PART II

Your Past Life Begins Now - Document The
Threat You Are Under

Now that I had my new identity created, and
had practiced a detailed backstory, I was ready to
let go of my old identity.

The first step was to make a video taped state-
ment which documented the threat I was under. I
sent digital copies of this video to the people I
trusted most. I also have a copy uploaded as a
private, password encrypted video on my Vimeo
channel. The password to the video is very clearly
written in my address book - so should something

ever happen, God forbid, and my murder was being investigated - detectives would easily be able to access this video and my killer would be brought to justice.

In this video, you must clearly explain you have a fear of being murdered or suicided. You must also explain in detail that you have a desire to live and that you would never commit suicide.

Next there are a serious of concepts you must address fully during the video. Start by explaining what individual you believe wants you dead. Explain why this person wants you dead. Give the names of anyone that can support your claim that this person is your enemy. This could be your trusted inner circle or it could be a history of police reports, court orders and legal proceedings. Either way, give corroborative evidence. Next, speculate as best you can how you think this person will murder you. If they have ever tried killing you in the past, explain the method they used. Again, now would be a good time to remind viewers you are definitely not suicidal. Talk about why you want to live. Then talk about what circumstances you would need to face in order to consider suicide. Next, address the fact that you do - or don't - abuse life threatening substances. Disclose if you have these substances in your home. Also disclose if you possess any lethal weapons and where you keep them. Explain your driving history - do you drive safely, have any record of traffic accidents or violations? It's ok if you do, just explain what happened in detail. Finally, explain if you have a desire to run away and flee your current home.

Once you document the threat you are under, you can breathe a sigh of relief knowing that this video may serve as a deterrent and may also serve as a tool for justice. Let's hope this video will never have to be watched by anyone! That's certainly my goal. Which is why I go to the lengths I do for my privacy.

Consider Your Proof Of Life

When creating your new life, you want to make sure that people from your old identity still think you are alive (which you are) but that you have just moved on (which you have). The last thing you want is any of these associates from your former life reporting you as missing - at which point your new life is exposed!

Consider drifting away from social media, but keeping a blog active that you post on perhaps once every month or two. Clearly, it's you still writing and maintaining your blog, but you are just taking some time for solitude.

The whole point is you need some sort of "proof of life" for everyone in your old world to not spend their time looking for you in the new one. This will vary greatly from reader to reader, so I suggest you take a moment to consider what documented "proof of life" you can use to your advantage which does not in any way threaten to expose the new life you are building.

Your Future Depends On Your Past

It's important to remember that your future depends on your past. More specifically, the success of your future life, depends on how you handle your past one.

Consider drifting away from your old associates but be careful to not cross contaminate your new life with folks from your past.

This is incredibly difficult and may take years to fully complete! You can not just go dark one day and disconnect from everyone in your past life - that will raise too many red flags and cause folks to start wondering about you. Rather, slowly burn away - like a candle slowly fading down.

At the same time, I do not advocate for being totally disconnected. Rather, I suggest you connect

- but on a new device with your new associates in your new life.

If you are starting a new life, hiding from the online world seems like a pretty safe move. However, that's not usually the case. Our world is connected digitally and you will blend in by hiding amongst the masses. Simply put, if your new identity has no existence online, you will really stick out like a sore thumb to your new associates. If a new neighbor or acquaintance meets you in your new life, they will Google your name. People are nosy and love to Google each other. If they get no results - that will cause them to wonder about you.

The last thing you want is for people in your new life to search out your old one!

See how complex this can become? It takes years of practice. But I know that if I can figure all this out, you can too!

Your New Physical Life - Privacy Tips For Banking And Finances

We will be dividing some of this book up between "physical life" and "digital life". By this I mean, what you do "off line" and "on line". Obviously, these worlds always cross, and that's fine, but for purposes of organization, I am labeling these tips and tricks under "physical" and "digital" lives.

Let's start with your basic everyday personal (and professional) finances.

You must use your bank as little as possible. This is essential. You never want to keep more than five hundred dollars in your bank account. Your low balance will act as a deterrent for large unauthorized withdrawals used in identity theft.

Your bank account should be a business account, not a personal one. You can create an LLC for this because you must bank under a business name. This really is a great step in making life difficult for your stalker. More on LLC's later in this book.

Of course, when you open up this new business bank account you will not be using your real home address. You will use any other address available to you other than your own. In a little bit, we'll discuss alternate addresses. You can not have your home address on file with your bank.

At this point, it goes without saying that paying for everything in all cash is absolutely essential for your privacy. If your entire life runs on a cash basis, no one you make purchases from will ever know your real name and identity. Furthermore, your bank will be unable to track your purchases and therefore be unable to sell your purchase history to advertisers. Stores where you made purchases from will also be unable to sell your information. If you use a credit, debit or bank card - all of your purchases are being tracked by multiple parties. It is also being sold over and over again.

Cash eliminates this problem immediately.

I recommend you have a cash reserve of five thousand dollars on hand at all times. This would be money you can use to flee and start over in a new city, state or even country. I know it is difficult to save that much money, but consider the alternative. Work hard. Try to get a cash reserve. The peace of mind it will give you is invaluable. Also - you can not ask your family for money should the s**t hit the fan and you need to flee. They will rat you out and disclose your new location. If you flee, you do so alone and you stay that way. I haven't had to fully flee, but I can do so at any point if I'm faced with that decision.

It goes without saying, but you also must stop using checks. You can pay all your bills by cash or with money orders.

In a little bit we will be discussing smartphones and computers. If you do online banking, that's fine, but it can only be done on new, secure devices. A device is secure only if its been in your hands and within your vision since the moment it was removed from its package. Can you really say your smartphone is secure? Has anyone else ever held it? Exactly. You must do your banking on a new device. My stalker was able to see everything I did on my phone because he cloned my phone to his. That meant he had my bank account number, password and log-in information, account balance and a detailed record of anything I purchased and everywhere I went - since I was still using my bankcard at the time.

Pay off and close all former credit cards. Do not use credit. I know it's tempting, but if you live your life on a cash basis you will be in less debt and be significantly more secure than the majority of citizens.

Finally, if you need a credit card to make a purchase online you can buy an anonymous debit card and load it with cash. A great one to use is a Simon Mall Card, but there are tons of options out there.

Privacy Tips For Housing And Utilities

Assuming you are starting a new life, you will

need a new home. If you are renting an apartment, never rent it in your name. Do not rent an apartment if you have to provide your landlord with your social security number.

Look for a landlord or leasing agency that accepts a corporate rental. It does not have to be a real corporation. You can set up an LLC quickly and use this company as a name for your lease. Explain that you are new to the area and setting up a new sales region and your company needs this apartment. Many landlords will be fine with this, but may just ask for an extra month of rent when you move in (which you'll get back when you move out).

Remember, once you've moved in - never, ever pay your rent by check! Send a money order. Always, send a money order.

All of your utilities must be listed under your business name as well. Explain that bills can not be paid if they aren't listed correctly under the business name. Also, make sure your bills are sent electronically or else to an alternate address.

You can not receive any mail at your new apartment. Period.

If the utility company wants your social security number, hang up, call again and work with another rep. You can not link your name or social security number to your new home.

If you have a peephole in your door, cover it immediately with tape. They make "peephole reversers" which sell online for very cheap. These devices can be used to easily look inside your apartment!

I installed a Ring doorbell camera inside my apartment which points at my door. Every time the door opens, my Ring doorbell camera records the action and saves the video to the cloud. The Ring doorbell camera was $99 and a year of service was $30. You do not need to ask your landlord if you can install one - it's the same as hanging a picture on your wall.

When I leave my apartment, I have a cheap AM/FM radio by the door which I play while I'm gone. I always keep several lights on when I'm away as well.

I do not have my name listed on my door or on my mailbox. This is great, because I get no mail at my mailbox. I listed a generic male's name on my door and mailbox.

When I moved in to my new apartment, I immediately changed the lock and key. I removed the cylinder, took it to a locksmith and had the combination changed. Now my landlord can not enter my apartment.

I have a paper shredder and I use it for all my paper trash.

I look at my home as my fortress and I want to fortify it as much as I possibly can. It is my sanctuary and my refuge.

Privacy Tips For Transportation

Walking or bicycling are the best modes for transportation to live a private life. You do not need a driver's license or insurance for either. You will be undetected in most scenarios. Also, it's cheaper than having a car, gives you a great workout and is better for our planet.

I understand walking or bicycling isn't for everyone, and you may have to have a car. If so, sell your current vehicle immediately and buy a new one - the least flashy one you can find. Something so average that even a gray rock would be ashamed to be seen in it.

When you buy your new car, be sure to buy it and register it under your business (LLC) name. Never purchase and register a vehicle under your own name.

You will need to show your drivers license to a police officer if you are ever stopped. If you rent a car, you will also need to show your drivers license. A passport can not be used as identification in either of these scenarios.

Car Insurance is a must, and it will have to be in your legal name (which I assume ties your new life to your old one). This isn't ideal, but there is no way to beat it.

Finally, a note about flying.

Your privacy goes completely out the window the moment you set foot in an airport. If you must fly - I recommend you never check any bags. It is a major security hazard and completely avoidable if you travel with a minimal amount of belongings.

Your New Digital Life - Privacy Tips For Phones, Computers And More

I had to destroy all of my old devices - an iPhone, an iPad tablet and a MacBook Pro laptop. All of them gone. I replaced them with lower quality devices which essentially do the same thing but for a fraction of the cost. If I need to throw them out again, it will be significantly less costly.

I no longer use a smartphone. It is too risky. There are also numerous studies which show that apps on your phone are always listening to you. I do not consider my freedom worth the trade for a fancy new smartphone.

At first I missed my smartphone, but now I would never want one. I purchased a cheap cell phone on Amazon that does nothing but make and take calls. No texts. There is no GPS so I am not being tracked through those means. I also have no apps. Finally, I purchased the three dollar a month pay as you go plan using cash at a T-Mobile store. I did not have to give them my name, social security number or provide any identification.

If I ever have to call 911 I will immediately throw this phone away. Police and emergency services will link my name with my phone number and then the process of being traced starts all over again.

I do not have a landline phone. If I did, it would be set up under a fake name or a fake business name. I would not pay to be unlisted because that is a scam - you pay more money to be "unlisted" - but your phone company still sells all your information to other third parties. So you are still "listed". Finally, I would never dial a "toll free" number - as soon as you call one from a landline your name, phone number and address are all linked together.

I would not carry a smartphone with me when I fly and I would not travel long distance by car or train with a smartphone. Why? There is no warrant needed to search all the contents of a smartphone.

If someone asks for my number, I give them any one of these possible digits: 909-661-0001 to 909-661-0090 and 619-364-0003 to 619-364-0090. These numbers will never be issued, but will always ring and the caller will hear a busy signal.

If you are a lady at a bar and a creepy guy asks for your number, I would give any one of the following numbers: 717-980-0000 to 717-980-9999. These numbers will never be issued, and the caller will be given a disconnected message when they call them.

As soon as I got my new laptop, I disabled its camera and microphone. I ran Decrap on my machine. I installed TOR and use that as my exclusive web browser. If there are some sites which I try visiting that do not function with TOR, I use Firefox while on Private Browsing Mode. I am not a hacker, nor am I particularly "techie" - but I was able to figure out how to use TOR as my web browser and you should too. There are thousands of books and countless articles on what TOR is, and I will leave that to the experts. Just trust me - you need to use it.

Now on to two very important points: avoid Google and Facebook like the plague!

First, I no longer use Google. For anything. It is a massive surveillance company and it can not be trusted. I changed my default search engine to DuckDuckGo. I can not use Gmail. All of my past Gmail and Google accounts - along with all of their contents - I permanently deleted. I now use Protonmail for my email service. It is fantastic. I deleted my YouTube channel and now use Vimeo instead. Other privacy books recommend creating Google Alerts to monitor your key data - like all of your old and new names, personas, addresses, phones and emails - which is a horrible tip because it immediately links old with new...on Google! Shockingly bad advice.

Finally, I will never use Facebook again. It too can not be trusted and its surveillance is shocking.

Eventually I will have two laptops. One will be my "clean" laptop that I will use when I travel. Meaning it could be taken and have its contents searched and nothing would link my identities. I would also have a "personal" laptop which would be under lock and key and never leave my house.

All of its contents would be on a USB drive I could destroy should I ever be subjected to a search.

Privacy Tips For Social Media And Facial Recognition

As I stated earlier in this book, I recommend your new identity have some sort of social media presence - however, you must make sure your new identity will never come in contact with your old life.

Therefore, either way, I will never join Facebook again. There is absolutely no privacy. Do not trust the privacy settings. Any "friend" can find your exact location as can any "friend of friends". Facebook is the number one way stalkers track their victims. I know Facebook is fun, but it is a major threat to your safety.

It is getting harder and harder to beat facial recognition and the technology is getting better and better. Eventually the technology will win the battle, but for now realize that there are a few tips you can try to use to beat facial recognition technology. They are: always wear a baseball cap, always wear tinted dark glasses, smile a lot, have some facial hair (if you are a man) and always look at your feet.

Finally - the best advice - simply avoid getting

your picture taken. That's really tough, but do your best to avoid it at all costs.

If you are posting photos or videos on social media, remember you must scrub all Exif Data from the video or picture before you upload it. Exif Data contains key information - often times including the precise GPS coordinates of where a photo or video was created. There are online Exif Data scrubbers you can use for free.

Privacy Tips For Email, Physical Mail And A Ghost Address

My first tip is to stop using Gmail immediately. Forever. Google is way worse than Facebook for privacy and shockingly unreliable if you travel frequently.

Protonmail is absolutely wonderful for security. It is also free and contains no ads.

I never reply to an email. There is data within a reply, such as an IP Address, which the recipient can use to discover your actual, physical address. Instead of replying to an email, I start a new fresh email and send my reply in that manner.

I avoid using snail mail (physical mail). If I have to send mail, I only do it from inside a post office. I never leave my outgoing mail in my apartments outgoing box or even in a blue mailbox on the street. Both can easily be broken into. I carry my mail inside the post office during office hours and hand the worker my outgoing letters. It's really annoying to have to do that, so I try to avoid using mail at all costs.

If you rent a PO Box you will need to provide two forms of identification. That's probably fine, but just be cautious. I would rent a PO Box as far from your real home as possible, and I would vary when I check my Box, always during office hours however.

Some states have an address confidentiality program which you may qualify for. I would look into this. It provides you with a federally recognized confidential PO Box to use as your main address on all legal documents at a federal and state level.

The point in all this, is that you can not send or receive any mail to or from your real home address. It is essential for your safety that your name not ever be connected to that home address. Which means, you can not have any mail linking the two.

This means I never get any deliveries to my house. No food deliveries. No Amazon package deliveries - I use an Amazon package dropbox location in a public building during office hours.

I use a fake return address and no name on all the mail I send in the spot where a return address goes. This prevents people from looking at my mail should they see my name and address on the upper left corner.

I would never give my home address to anyone. Including my lawyer, CPA, bank, doctor, dentist, college, family or friends. Even my close family does not know my address.

If I ever receive a piece of unwanted mail at my home address I put a sticker on the envelope that says "Not deliverable as addressed, unable to forward". That sticker is placed over the address, but not covering my name. I black out all bar codes on the envelope. I draw an arrow pointing back to the return address. I send that back at a post office not located in my own zip code. This little trick is a great way to get your name and address removed from tons of databases all over the world.

There are many great books on the subject of privacy that call for the getting of a physical ghost address - which is a street address that is not connected to you but which you can still receive mail at. I find them all to be quite complex and the pursuit of a ghost address pretty stressful. I personally would start with my state's address confidentiality program and see where that takes me. I would also try to get as much of my mail delivered to me electronically. The days of needing a physical mailing address seem to be numbered in my opinion.

PART III

Build Your Own Safe-house - The Safe-house Circle

I like to think of my new life as a safe-house that have built for myself. This safe-house is strong and secure. Around it, there is an invisible circle.

Visible from my new circle, is my old one. In that invisible circle is my past life. That circle contains my stalker. It also contains all of my old associates and everything from my past. My stalker's tactic will be to search through this circle - because it is the only one he knows. He will hunt through phone records, finances, talk to old friends and family members and see if there's any leads that can shed some light on where I am now living.

The goal is to keep both these circles separate. Old Circle can not know about New Circle, and New Circle can not know about Old Circle. They must stay disconnected. As soon as the circles meet - the new life I have built is compromised and I must start all over again, building yet another new life. I can not ever let any of my past pierce my present circle. If the circles ever connect - it will lead to my demise.

In short, always be aware of the connections you have made - and the ones you are making today. Question if your past can connect to your present, and therefore ruin your future.

Sanctuary In Deception

There is sanctuary in deception. You must become a master in the fine art of deceiving the people you have left behind in your past life. You will use deception to lead your stalker astray. That is the purpose of deception. If you do not create misinformation and keep them busy following leads, they will use their time to search for your real new life information which could potentially lead your stalker to your safe-house.

Targeted Deception is a detailed and very well

planned technique to make it appear like you live and have built a new life in a specific city - but all of the information within your targeted deception plan is false. The city and the new life you have built is false. Make this new life so real that your stalker must follow up all leads - and if you are successful, they will be so busy tracking you down in this false life that they will never even think to find your real one!

Consider Multiple Identities

You may wish to consider using multiple identities for various aspects of your new life. I already mentioned that I do this. It's a very successful tool which also compartmentalizes the facets of your world. If one identity is ever compromised, I can sever my ties with that identity and only need to replace one small aspect of my life. If my entire life is built on one new identity and it becomes compromised, then I must sacrifice my entire new life and build an entire new identity. Not fun!

For example: if people at your painting class know you as "Lisa" and people at your church know you as "Jane" then if your stalker somehow discovers your painting class he will only know the "Lisa" identity. "Jane" (and all the new connections you've made at church) are still totally safe. It's a lot easier to rebuild one aspect of your life than your entire life.

Consider how many identities you need based upon the threat you feel you are under. Only you can make this judgment.

Practical Preparedness: Be Ready At All Times - On Person Essentials

Over the years I have taken great comfort in being prepared at all times. I am prepare to leave the new life I have built and start completely over from scratch at any moment. Believe me, I don't want to do this - but if I have to, I can and will.

How prepared are you to leave and start over fresh?

I keep five hundred dollars cash on my person at all times. I also have my passport. I personally think those two elements are enough to get me started on a new journey. What do you need to carry with you on your person so that you are prepared for a new adventure if the s**t really hits the fan?

Your Everyday Carry Kit

There are many pre-made "everyday carry kits" available to purchase online. I built mine myself. I never leave home without my Primary EDC (every day carry). It is in old Altoids tin and contains the following:

1.Cell phone (I told you it was small and very generic)

2. USB drive with my entire business and financial information on it

3.HD card with a backup of the USB drive

4.HD card that is empty

5.Five hundred dollars

That is what is in my Primary EDC. I always have that Altoids tin on me along with my passport. I also have a Secondary EDC. I bring this with me if I feel like I may be gone from the house for more than an hour or two. This kit is larger and goes in my backpack. It contains the following:

1.Multi-Tool (Leatherman)

2.LED Flashlight

3.Matches and Lighter

4.Pocket First Aid Kit

5.Para-cord

6.Mini Pry-bar

7.Small notebook and pencil

This kit just brings me a little bit of extra comfort, knowing that should I need any of those items, they are on me at all times.

Your Bug Out Bag

About a year ago I started to build my own "Bug Out Bag", which is defined as *a portable kit that normally contains the items one would require to survive for at least 72 hours when evacuating from a disaster, although some kits are designed to last for a longer period.*

I am not a professional survivalist, but I have done a lot of research on Bug Out Bags. Below is a list of what mine contains - again this is based upon what brings me comfort and peace of mind. Your bag may be different. Here's what is in mine:

1. Alcohol prep pads
2. Antibiotics
3. Band-aids and mole-skin pads
4. Bandanna
5. Batteries (rechargeable)
6. Blood clotting sponge
7. Body warmer packets
8. Calorie dense food bars (24 bars, 2000 calories per bar)
9. Camo Face Paint Sticks
10. Collapsible bowl (stainless steel)
11. Compass
12. Daily multivitamins
13. Dental floss
14. Duct tape

15. Electrical tape

16. Fishing line (braided)

17. Fishing pole (pocket sized)

18. Freeze dried meals (24 packs of beef stroganoff)

19. Glasses (a backup pair)

20. Glow sticks

21. Hand crank radio (AM/FM/Digital)

22. Hand sanitizer

23. Hatchet

24. Headlamp (LED)

25. Hook, swivel, sinker set (for fishing)

26. Hydrogen peroxide

27. Insect repellent

28. Knife (and sharpener)

29. Lighter

30. Magnifying glass (small)

31. Mirror (for signaling)

32. Moist towelettes

33. Mosquito head net

34. Multi Tool (with pliers)

35. Neosporin

36. Notepad and pencil

37. Pain killers (generic)

38. Para-cord

39. Pepper Spray

40. Q-Tips (cotton swabs)

41. Rain poncho with hood

42. Safety pins

43. Sewing kit

44. Shovel (compact, folding)

45. Sleeping bag

46. Sleeping pad

47. Snare wires

48. Soap

49. Socks and underwear

50. Solar charger

51. Spork (titanium, spoon-fork)

52. Stocking cap

53. Stun Gun

54. Sun screen

55. Sunglasses (prescription)

56. Super glue

57. Surgical tape

58. Survival gloves

59. Survival hammock

60. Survival Slingshot

61. Survival watch

62. Tactical flashlight

63. Takedown Survival Bow (with arrows)

64. Tampons

65. Tarp shelter

66. Topographical maps

67. Tweezers and nail clippers

68. Vaseline

69. Water bottle (stainless steel)

70. Water filter (portable)

71. Water purification tablets

72. Waterproof storage container

73. Waterproof survival matches

74. Whistle

75. Wire saw (small)

76. Wound gauze roll

77. Zip ties

I do not consider myself to be paranoid, but having this kit in my bedroom closet brings me a lot of comfort. I know that with my Primary and Secondary Everyday Carry Kits, along with my Bug Out Bag that I could grab my entire life in less than five seconds and be out the door and on my way to creating a new world for myself.

Making Money Anonymously - Build Your Secret Business

You may be wondering what I do to earn money. Obviously you need to have a job to support yourself while you build a new life.

I decided to sacrifice my lucrative and very public career to protect my privacy and personal safety. That is why I built a secret business and I now make all of my money anonymously.

This was very hard to do and took almost a year before I saw any profit. I actually run several small businesses anonymously. My thinking is that if one business ever were to be compromised I can quickly let it go and have others in place that are still actively earning money.

I do not work for anyone. I only work for myself. This is very important because if I worked for someone else I would have to comply with their rules - and I guarantee that they would have a primary goal of making money. Protecting my privacy would most likely not be a goal of my boss. So I became my own boss and made each of these goals equally important: *I need to make money and protect my privacy.* I do this by building my anonymous businesses.

I run my businesses almost 100% online. I do not need to meet in person with any potential clients, nor do I need to speak on the phone or have video conferencing calls. If a client wants to speak on the phone, I politely tell them I am deaf. No one I work for ever really knows who they are working with. I do not need to go anywhere specific, because my businesses can be run from inside my home. If I am "hired" by someone it is as an Independent Contractor and based upon my own terms and conditions for my safety.

All payments to my businesses are made online. I do not receive checks by mail.

The reason I started each of my businesses was for privacy and for profit. The two go hand in hand.

Tips To Create A Secret LLC

With each new business I start, I form a secret LLC which has a very, very generic business name. Nothing flashy, something so generic you would have a hard time searching for it online.

LLC stands for "Limited Liability Company". It is defined as *the US specific form of a private limited company. It is a business structure that can combine the pass-through taxation of a partnership or sole proprietorship with the limited liability of a corpora-tion. An LLC is not a corporation in and of itself; it is a legal form of a company that provides limited liability to its owners in many jurisdictions.*

You will want an LLC. Probably multiple LLC's. They are very easy to set up and do not require much cash.

All of my businesses are filed in Wyoming because I will be unnamed as an Owner. This is because Wyoming LLC's do not show ownership in the Articles Of Organization. I hire a company to serve as my Registered Agent. I use that company's address as my ghost address for the LLC.

The name of my LLC never appears on any State or Federal Tax returns. I report earnings and expenses on Schedule C with my personal 1040 tax return. I pay all my taxes and strongly advise that you do the same. Do not mess with the IRS - just be a good citizen and file your taxes. Pay them. It's just part of living in the greatest country on earth.

I can create a new LLC this way for each new business. I can even create a new LLC to buy cars, houses or land.

Streams Flow Into Rivers: Money Sources

As I have stated earlier, I feel it is important to create multiple revenue streams - so I have created several small businesses. I like to think of each business as a steady stream which flows into the river that is my new life. Each stream is not very significant, but when combined - they form a very stable new beginning.

And that is what this book has been about: new beginnings.

I implore you to consider the tips and tricks I have learned in my own journey. I will keep pursuing my quest for privacy, because I value my own personal freedom.

It's funny. I started this crazy adventure because of a very, very negative experience. Now that I am away from the immediate danger and the threat has passed, I can breathe again. I can look back at what I have learned and realized that in a strange way I am almost thankful for my stalker. If it wasn't for him I would not be where I am today.

And where is that?

I am a gray rock, finding safety in the shadows. I know that I have built a new life for myself on my own terms and this life is very safe and secure. My privacy is my freedom and I am so blessed to have earned this new life.

I know you are capable of taking back your world too. Start small. You do not need to accomplish all of this at once. Slowly keep revisiting my book and others like it. I believe in you and I want you to remember this one infallible truth: *you deserve to feel safe at all times!*

In 2019, the Jack and Kitty Norton released a memoir called *Two Stalkers One Goal*. In a story stranger than fiction, the inspiring book offers hope and healing for victims of stalking, cyber-stalking, narcissistic abuse, gossip and bullying... all with more twists and turns than any Hollywood thriller.

Jack's latest book, *Cornstars: Rube Music In Swing Time*, is a sweeping overview of American musical entertainment set in the later days of minstrelsy through the early days of television. It was nominated for the 2021 Association for Recorded Sound Collections Awards for Excellence in Historical Recorded Sound Research.

Earlier in their career, Jack and Kitty co-created, co-directed, co-wrote and co-starred in *The Zinghoppers Show*, a children's television series which earned six regional Emmy Award nominations for Nashville Public Television and was broadcast on over 150 PBS member stations nationwide and in 175 countries on the AFN Family Channel and on Trinity Broadcast Network. Four original songs written and performed by Jack and Kitty Norton were featured in the Oscar nominated Willem Dafoe film *The Florida Project* (A24) by director Sean Baker (Tan-

gerine) which debuted at the 49th edition of
Cannes Directors' Fortnight as part of the Cannes
Film Festival.

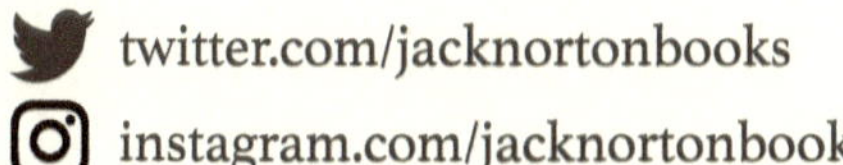

DISCLAIMER

information in this book. However, neither the authors nor the publisher assumes any responsibility for errors, omissions, or contrary interpretations of the content within.

Do you research before posting anything online. This information is intended for entertainment use, consists of opinions, and should not be constructed as legal advice or business guidance. Neither the authors nor the publisher can be responsible for any content that you choose to post online nor loss of income. Again, this book is for entertainment purposes only, and so the views of the authors should not be taken as expert instructions or commands. The reader is responsible for his or her own actions. Adherence to all applicable laws, including but not limited to international, federal, state and local regulations is the sole responsibility of the purchaser or reader.

This book may contain reference links to other relevant content. Neither the authors nor the publisher can be responsible for content posted on other sites.

Neither the authors nor the publisher assumes any responsibility or liability on behalf of the purchaser or reader of this book.

Thank you to all my friends that connected with me on JackAndKitty.com - you gave me the push I needed to write this book. And thank you to my best friend and soulmate, Kitty. I'll love you forever and beyond.

* 9 7 9 8 2 0 1 7 4 0 6 6 5 *